# Goddess of
Glass Mountains

*poems by*

# Madronna Holden

*Finishing Line Press*
Georgetown, Kentucky

# Goddess of
# Glass Mountains

Copyright © 2021 by Madronna Holden
ISBN 978-1-64662-617-5 First Edition
All rights reserved under International and Pan-American Copyright Conventions.
No part of this book may be reproduced in any manner whatsoever without written permission from the publisher, except in the case of brief quotations embodied in critical articles and reviews.

## ACKNOWLEDGMENTS

"All I Can See from Here" and "Autumn/Libra" as contest winners in *Pacifica* (1996).
"The Revolution below Us" in *Green Fuse* (1997)
"Do Not Worry about the Dry Season" in the anthology, *Dona Nobis Pacem* (2006)
"Advice from an Iris" and "If You Could Tell Your Story with Wings" in the *Clackamas Literary Review* (2019)
"As Picasso Turned the World to Glass" and "If the World Were a Literal Thing" in *Poemeleon* (2020)
"Dreams of Sand and Bears" in *The Bitter Oleander* (2020) and was also chosen as poem of the day by *Verse Daily*.

Publisher: Leah Huete de Maines
Editor: Christen Kincaid
Cover Art: 'Hoop of Truth',©2020, Mara Friedman: newmoonvisions.com
Author Photo: Risa Holden
Cover Design: Elizabeth Maines McCleavy

Order online: www.finishinglinepress.com
also available on amazon.com

Author inquiries and mail orders:
Finishing Line Press
PO Box 1626
Georgetown, Kentucky 40324
USA

# Table of Contents

Meditation for Knowing What You Want ................................ 1
Badger Medicine ........................................................................ 2
Advice from an Iris .................................................................... 4
Goddess of Glass Mountains .................................................... 5
As Picasso Turned the World to Glass .................................... 6
If the World Were a Literal Thing ........................................... 7
The Glass in My Eye ................................................................. 8
Fire Muse ................................................................................... 9
Combustible ............................................................................. 10
Wearing the Marrow .............................................................. 11
The Poet Jumps the Line ....................................................... 13
List of Mysterious Things ...................................................... 14
Yes, the Universe is Expanding ............................................. 15
Autumn/Libra ......................................................................... 16
All I Can See from Here ........................................................ 18
Fractal ...................................................................................... 19
The Girl Who Came to Symphonies .................................... 20
Iron Island ............................................................................... 22
Some Things I Don't Know About My Country ................ 23
Scabs on the Moon ................................................................. 24
Lullaby for the Forgotten ...................................................... 26
Dreams of Sand and Bears .................................................... 28
The Revolution below Us ...................................................... 29
Don't Go Yet ........................................................................... 31
How Our Dreams Pray for Us .............................................. 32
To Flower in the Rain ............................................................ 33
If You Could Tell Your Story with Wings ........................... 34
Do Not Worry about the Dry Season .................................. 35

## Meditation for Knowing What You Want

Stand in the rain.

(In a drought
your own tears
will have to do.)

Moisten your hands,
singing to water:
the song the river
answers you with
is the song
of your desire.

Sing it to the passion
rumbling in the time before time
that invented your body.

In between what erupts there
something else sinks down.
settling in your heart.

Keep it for yourself.

Ask yourself once more
what it is you desire—
and wait for life
to answer you.

**Badger Medicine**

Be inevitable.

Fight like the sun
fights for the day.

Get everything
to open its eyes
before you.

Melt something:
let it run, like honey,
binding the wound,
leaving behind only
the tribute of bees
the memory of flowers.

Suck out the poison.

Persist.

Do not give up
because you have told yourself
to give up.

(Do not repeat to yourself
how many things can go wrong).

All secrets have storms in their eyes:
go there: moan the hurricane aloud,
honor that which asks to be sung
with your own voice;
fling it back into the wind
as beauty, thanking it
for the gift.

Dance like a branch in the wind,
your energy running up from the land,
carrying light in your arms,
landing on your roots.

Stay close to the earth
against the danger of being lost.
Listen to her seasons to know
when to sleep inside and dream,
and when to reach out.

Refuse to disappear.

Talk to the soul you are working
to bring back:

(Talk to your own soul)

Whisper how
the world needs it.

Do not give up.

Fight this way to bring
every spirit home

(To bring your own spirit home)

Because there is no other way,
because it is our task
to learn how to love
in every lifetime.

**Advice from an Iris**

Don't blame the sirens
who happened to be singing
to their Mother Ocean
when your boat came along.

What you took for wreckage
was only beauty holding its own
like the Oregon iris
named *tenax*/tenacity,
since ropes braided from it
cannot be broken

(They are ropes that
keep their promises).

True, their bloom
might dizzy the compasses
of passers-by with their
sweet surprises.

True, they might turn
forest shadows purple
as accused

And their tongues spark
with tiny white stars eager
to tell you everything

But you can't blame the flowers
for your own flowered tongue.

Your song heard
by the sea whether
or not passers-by
tie themselves up
against hearing it.

Your own story
that would proclaim itself
by blooming.

**Goddess of Glass Mountains**

The goddess of junkyards
tells me to give her each thing
I want to get rid of.

She will compost
my wasted moments
where a tree can eat them
and grow greener—

spill out my watery choices
where a river can drink
them and run freer

set out those things
that might have been useful
had I ever used them
where sunlight can work on them
until no one (not even me)
recognizes them for the folly
they once were.

Dear goddess of garbage heaps,
I would give you everything—
have you strip me so
I can float on your air—

While I learn
how to ascend
your glass mountains

without sliding
backwards

turning to salt

or losing someone I love
to the underworld.

## As Picasso Turned the World to Glass

He insisted the moment of creation
should be private as sex—
since you can only make an
object of power by going
underground
with it.

For him haunting was an
exact science. He placed
ghost-sheets over what
was missing, what
was fractured
or beheaded—

setting every piece in precise
pattern so as to make the
eyes ache with second
sight, the palms itch
with the urge
to rebuild.

## If the World Were a Literal Thing

If the world were a literal thing
my memory could not
describe you in oranges
and satin.

There would be none of this
business of suggestion
between my eyes
and yours.

My skin would be a guardhouse
without a gate, never opening
anything between us.

There would be no sly music
drifting seductively off key,
no voice with its ardent
imprecise hope.

The rain would be forbidden
from falling like smoke
against the far horizon.

I would live on my island
and you yours, the captured
moon making no overtures
to a tide between us.

We would have nothing
to quench our thirst
but the cider of certainty
pressed from apples
that can be neither
eaten nor planted.

There would be nothing
to tempt us—and nothing
to teach us.

**The Glass in My Eye**

I wear a clotted star in my eye:
when it first fell to me
it blazed and raged,
turning my sight to blood
and lightning.

It went away blinking,
leaving behind a white hole—
trap door to the blank score
of heaven.

Now even tears cannot wash it away—
this seeing so clearly
that which is not here.

I am forever scarred
by surplus light—
as through my starry eye
another world
keeps watch
on this one.

**Fire Muse**

Desire is written on the air, penetrating your breath with its incense.

Your words are spinning into red shadows, blooming petal by petal.

It seems a lifetime ago she led you to her room at the top of the stair where she reclined before you, spilling your years from her black hair.

She put a record on her limping turntable as fire brightened her room more insistently red.

There were maps of trenches on the wall, a worn helmet on its stand, the uniform you slipped out of.

(But how much of this mattered once sex got your attention?)

All these years later I want to ask, *have we been as blinded by the heat as by the light?*

**Combustible**

Your eyes glow
like the eyes of a cat
more patient
than I am.

You sizzle toward me—
tinder breathless
with waiting

casting off sparks
petal by petal

but you know I can't
come any closer

lest we catch fire

and burn together
until there is nothing
left of us

but our skin's idea
of enlightenment.

**Wearing the Marrow**
*(On going naked beyond the bone)*

If the universe is born in fire
and we are partners in the flame—
is that naked enough?

Down to the marrow—
is that what you mean—

Down to the mighty ocean inside the bones,
the light dissolved in the pearl,
the answer of belonging asked
so fast, we don't have time
for the inevitable questions
that follow

as we suck the custard
that can only be eaten
with the spoon of desire?

(What is left besides
the color of death
after the gate of flesh
is eaten away)

Or is it saltwater lapping us
downward until we can only
go to the shore of one another
absent of all else—including
where we have been—

as I become the wine
and you the glass that holds it
and I the hand that pours it
and you the hand that lifts it—
until when we drink,
we can't tell whose thirst
this is.

But only belief is that naked,
and her sister, hope—

only an offering made
once and for all
on the altar of intimacy.

(the original bargain with life
that brings us here)

And I am not capable
of such stellar nakedness—
I can only wear your touch
as trees wear their leaves
and the river wears stone,
taking such a long sweet
time at it.

As cinnamon wears its scent,
and cayenne its hot tongue—

as music wears its sound—

As I wear my mornings with the
lingering taste of dreams—
losing all distinction
between the world's nakedness
and my own.

**The poet jumps the line**

She knows there are riptides
out there: how cold the sea is
and how it runs to salt.

She has seen this shore
drowned daily

(Watched a hundred
fishermen carry away
their empty nets)

But she jumps anyway
as if there were no line
between this and that

(As if all the world were one)

She leaps, her arms full
of rhymes and hope:

Someone has told her this story
sung to her dreams
and now she knows
only this leaping
can save her.

**List of Mysterious Things**

Hands smaller than the daylight,
words forking over the darkness,
frogs louder than the sound of water,
a river in love with time
flowing away as you
put your hand in it.

Seeds prepared for waiting,
candles still to be lit,
nuts cracked open
by a creature whose language
you have yet to learn.

A mountaintop with one
naked remainder of a tree
scoured bright by wind and sun,
silvered in homage
to an unnamed god
of time.

**Yes, the Universe Is Expanding**

That which precedes the speed of light
is the instant antenna of the heart.

The black holes of the universe
are penetrated by longing
that breaks all the rules

obliterating the distance
between you and I

as our souls shake loose rumors
that predate the stars—

as we ascend the mountain of breath
on which matter becomes skin
and energy becomes desire—

and we wait there,
wait there

for light to catch up.

**Autumn/Libra**

Now you are sitting
with the lion's head in your lap,
his yellow curls running out
in all directions.

Now you are walking, carefully,
so carefully, in your gymnasium of sky:
with so many miles between
its touchstones of light.

But look!
into each of your footprints
is rushing a bandage of light.

Now you are floating, floating,
a sweet seed in your
parchment boat
on a sea so quiet
all you can do
is give your breath
to the ocean.

Now you are rolling, rolling,
over, over, through
the brown autumn thistle grass
that is the thread of crickets
weaving songs on their legs;
and you are rolling over, over,
into the place leaves tuck themselves:
in the glove of the wind.

So that after you have fallen, fallen,
along this swelling of the earth
you have a pocket full
of painted tears.

And now the lion's limb
is the trunk of a tree,
planted in this vast earth.

And the ocean's breath
is what you are breathing

(Remember?)

And now space, space is your
mantle and when you shake
your skin everything around you
dances to the bells of light.

And now the leaves
are clown's lace
and the moon is climbing steadily,
riding she-backed
on the old mare who knows.

**All I can see from here**

Is Raven coming toward us,
a black fume of laughter
from the world we dare not dismiss,

Raven, coming, coming,
hopping her way here from peg to peg
on her invisible line over the earth,

(Under her there is a great wheel:
if we could see it, we would know
why time never apologizes.)

We would know what Hawk
has promised the sky
as he lifts a shaman's body
into flight.

Dancing, his arms are a nest of wings,
sweeping the rug of dreams.
and all the while Frog
sits large-eyed, legs bent
toward transformation.

All I can see from here
is the one earth we share:
all I can see from this earth
is the crescent mouth of the moon
blowing out its visible loop of breath,
breathing the world white, white,
slick and soft as a promise.

All I can feel from here
is this sweet white wound of breathing:
and when you catch your breath
just there against my telling,
my story takes a sudden turn
so that there is a real woman
under the soft storm of your desire.

**Fractal**

For the girls eating oranges
it is all about the juice,
but they are dissipating orange peels
to waiting crows

whose wings increase
the intelligence of the wind
by hundreds of feathers.

## The Girl Who Came to Symphonies

She came alone,
sliding into the seat beside me.

Smoothing her wide-eyed pinafore,
she told me how she heard
the finishing note:
the note laid on the air
as a promise that played
in her mind forever.

(I thought of sunshine
and salt, of a child carrying
the tide in her basket
of shells.)

She showed me her season tickets,
turning them over and over
in her small hand
the color of glass—

But at the next performance she was gone.

I wonder if she heard
the final clash of the cymbals
wherever she was—

or only the whine and screech
of the train on which the orchestra
pulled out of town,
its cars rattling like coins
disappearing down
a storm drain.

If she knew her own absence
as a violin string waiting
to be plucked—

a single hair falling
from its root that makes
such a quiet sound
in each of us.

**Iron island**

I don't know if you ever
saw a foundry, smelled
melting metal

or came that close
to burning.

(that close to boiling over
and dissolving)

Or whether someone
looming over you
like a floating island
held you as you tried
to struggle away.

But you were terrified
by the folktale
of the iron island
that seduced passing ships
and held them there

unable to cry for help.

You don't remember
the rest of the story
since for you everything
stopped there.

## Some Things I Don't Know about My Country

I don't know why some
who claim to have seen
the face of God seek to
gun down everything
larger than themselves.

I don't know why we lose a child
to a gunshot wound every two hours
in these United States of America.

I can't recite
the names of the dead,
much less the list of all
they will never see
while the birds go on
celebrating the air.

And I don't know how it helps
when we rush into our days
with the abandon of drunken lovers,
as if feeling things ten times over
makes up for what some
will never feel again.

**Scabs on the Moon**
    *(For Esther)*

      I
If we all dreamt your way,
we could not help but notice
the sky's imperfect skin—
the blemishes pitting
our romantic moonglow.

Our dreams would be
naked and counting,
stymied by the splayed lumber
in our minds

as we forget our lines
before full houses
of onlookers.

      II
It's dangerous work,
you tell me, getting it free—
that log jam in your brain.

So you busy yourself instead
emptying cupboards of clean plates
to wash and wash again,
whisking away visitor's jackets
to fold into safe drawers.

### III
I am another visitor
hanging onto my jacket
as you grip my hands
and assure me you are
no longer hoping
to get it right.

It's gone beyond that—
but maybe you can
just point out those
scabs on the moon
for me to notice.

### IV
Meaning sets us down here
in the mud of life,
where we learn to recognize ourselves
in clay fired by time.
Sometimes we grow glazed and firm
and finished—have so much earth
in us we can dive right into the next world
on our roundness and our depth.

But sometimes our bowl
of meaning cracks—
fires us to our
loosened selves

as our wounds are displayed
by heaven to the whole watching
world below.

Then we can only
hold one another's hands
until the sky stops bleeding.

## Lullaby for the Forgotten

> *"Always and everywhere bring back everything lost"* —Carolyn Forchè

### I

There are those who would steal
the words of the dead.

But the words of the dead
are the words of the dead
forever.

### II

Those we have forgotten
sleep with Baba Yaga,
where they grow
eccentric and terrifying,
full of enchantment
and ghostly survival
in her hut that walks
on chicken legs,
lit by candles
of the skull.

In her dark wood
of price and balance
Baba Yage demands
that we pick up every grain
spilled from the sack of life.

For each seed we miss
Baba Yage rages in the voice
of the hurricane,
the burnt words
of the firestorm,
the cracked words
of the earthquake.

Words kept in the chicken castle
of the old woman fatten themselves
on wildness—fling themselves
at us with claw and fang, fur and fat,
turning some men into goats—
and nations to sand.

Baba Yaga can only be pacified
with a lullaby for the forgotten—
whose words do not speak
unless they sing, do not sing
unless they sing the world closer.

Words so supple
they cannot be broken.
words so round
they cannot be cornered,
words so fluid
they run out
between prison bars

slipping under
the very eye
of the captain
of the guard

freeing everything.

    III
To recover the words of the lost
is to the raise the dead:
to perform an act of God.

### Dreams of Sand and Bears
*(On reading Khaled Hosseini's A Thousand Splendid Suns)*

In the mountains that watch over these sands
a bear sleeps wrapped in her furry dreams.

In the bear's religion everything
will ripen when she wakes.

But what can the faith of bears do
against loaded rifles and empty kettles?

What can the dreams of mountains do
against crumbling mud shelters?

They have not stopped the man's hand
on the wooden door to the room
where two girls lie huddled—
their feet long since
hardened on sand.

They will soon be roused
for their journey

whether or not they know
their price in lamb and salt

or the names of the streets
in the city that will lose them

or how their father will find his way
in his own sleep again after
he sells his daughters—

as the mountains tremble
with the growl in their dreams.

## The Revolution Below Us

I want to tell you
how the daffodils are ready
to risk the sun and the crocuses
have opened their mouths to the rain,
swallowing the purple sky.
I want to tell you
there is that gypsy warmth
in the air, and we could go naked
like you remember.

But you are where children
ride llamas into revolution.
Children! Llamas!

Where there are a thousand small
houses with their doors closed,
each hiding a hero
the army comes to steal away,
door by door, root
by root.

I want to tell you that here
the sky has turned cinnamon,
dived into an ocean of smell
and brought up apricot
and apple blossoms
that have not forgotten
how to hope.

But I cannot find you among
the thousand horses that stagger
in the dust between us, bearing
their riders into vision so hungry
it eats itself.

You ride among mountains and jungles
I can only imagine,
pyramids that stack immense time
against the sky,
women who weave their own eyes
into the clothing they place
on each of their kin
like a sacrament.

Strange country, I ask you,
like a lover, to come into my skin.
Your ocean beats its same heart
on this shore; our weather migrates
up from you, covering the earth
with your voices in the music
of wind and birds, falling to us
with that same heat that opens
the heart of the daffodils,
the hunger of the crocuses
among us.

**Don't Go Yet**

Your body is unhinging
its mother cells one by one
as your breath becomes
the liquor of breath
entwined in
sea lungs.

I am counting it
with my heartbeats.

*Don't go yet,*
*not yet, not yet.*

Talk to me in the language
from another time

in the words of fallen leaves
lifting back to their branch.

Tell me how rivers burn
with light before
they become water,

how mountains kneel
in the fire of the land
yet to be.

*I know you want to comfort me*

When you tell me
this red sun you leave behind
won't explode

(It is just eating a little dust)

You only want to console me
when you tell me
that the planter's hand
is always an earthquake
to the seed.

**How Our Dreams Pray for Us**

Our dreams are feathers
reciting prayers for wings.

They dress in our most vivid selves
to the get the attention
of the gods

chanting ciphers for the sake
of the music sleeping in the silence
from which song emerges—
for the sake of the light
leading night to morning.

They pray that an old woman still
sets beauty on the altar of her years,
an old man still envisions rainbows
on the mantel of his tired shoulders—

that a child still dreams alongside
mountains.

They pray with everything they have
that we never forget ourselves—
holding their prayerful hands
on our hearts

and their vision before our eyes.

## To flower in the rain

To flower in the rain
takes such faith:
to expose your tender
petals to the
thunderstorm.

Hope that one bee
will fly to you
on its own sodden wings,
risking everything
so that the fruit within you
may ripen

And you may do some good
in this world.

**If you could tell your story with wings**

If you could tell your story with wings
my sky would be larger
than it is now

(Though the mountains
would still know how
to find us.)

A story like that would warm us
in our nest until we peered
over the edge and fell
into flying

Our arms stretching
into the softness of clouds
our legs hitching a ride
on the wind

Such a story might
make everything count
as we passed among
the otherwise unnumbered
stars

Make everything
more than imagination

as it gathered us
into its words

Then we wouldn't be
stumbling, but practicing
on the path to heaven

We wouldn't be crying
but bringing rain
to the land.

## Do Not Worry about the Dry Season

Do not worry about the dry season:
there is a lake in the center of your hands
that contains the entire universe
of wonder and desire.

There is a world
coming to drink from that lake
so full of souls
it banishes every word
for *loneliness*
or *undone*.

The angels of your desire
will show you
how much your life
is worth.

How everything possible
becomes the dream
of itself, materializing
from your prayer.

Your body remembers everything.

Arise, say good morning
to the bells of your life.

Something has been saved
from every house of woman
ever burned:

Something pulled to shore
from every continent of human life
gone down in dark water:

Something has been saved
for you to come home to:
held forever in the words
you alone can speak to life.

**M**adronna Holden spent her childhood in the Arizona desert—with summer breaks at the farming home of her Czech grandparents in Iowa, who modeled their reverence for the land with stories told in the lyrical lilt of their native language. She holds a Ph.D. with a combined emphasis in anthropology and philosophy and has taught anthropology, philosophy, psychology, and mythology at universities in the US and abroad. She has been a long-time resident of the Pacific Northwest, where she has been the grateful guest of many indigenous elders. As well as a teacher, she has been a professional storyteller, a beekeeper, and an herbalist who guides ethnobotany walks at the local Arboretum—but always a poet, whose poetry surfaced to win her the Pacifica Prize for two years running and to inspire her play in poetic text, *The Descent of Inanna*, produced numerous times in collaboration with a talented director, musician, and troupe of local actors.

She has also authored several essays in mythology for Parabola and her non-fiction was a finalist in *Cutthroat*'s 2019 Barry Lopez contest.

Today her poetry is taking its rightful center stage in her life. She sees it as akin to shamanistic healing, opening the door to the other worlds that sustain and give dimension to ordinary reality, locating bits of soul that might otherwise be lost to us and singing them back home, bandaging our wounds by means of compassionate attention to what our dreams remember as we make allies with language.

And always, teaching us perspective by teaching us to laugh at ourselves.